CW00743156

SMASH THE HABIT
16 STEPS TO A NEW LIFE

KUL MAHAY

All rights reserved.

ISBN: **1515295923**
ISBN-13: **978-1515295921**

DEDICATION

To all of those who have lived with one debilitating habit or another. Those who suffer in silence and are simply waiting to break free and transform their lives.

CONTENTS

ACKNOWLEDGMENTS

To all of my clients past, present and future who have sparked the realisation in me that all of our behaviours, thoughts and actions are the results of our habits.

You have inspired me to write this book in the hope that many others will transform their lives as you have done (or will do) with yours.

Thank you.

Introduction

*"Nobody gets to live life backward. Look ahead!
That is where your future lies."*

Ann Landers

We all know how hard bad habits are to get rid of. They can range from the kind of habit that your partner or those closest to you moan at you about, like nail biting, to the more serious situations where the habit leads to addiction and dependency.

It's something that can play on your mind and affect your self-esteem or happiness, as you feel that you have lost control over your behaviour or, worse still, you are threatening your health, wealth and relationships.

Fear not!! There is a way of getting your own life back again and taking control over where it's heading. There is a way to smash that habit!

The key to it is that you have to **want** to have

control of your life in the first place. It is all too easy for us to say things like, 'It's just the way I am,' or 'I've been doing it too long to be able to change now.' Nonsense!

I've dealt with so many clients who have been in the same mindset regarding some kind of addictive behaviour that they have nurtured over several years. I've dealt with chocoholics, alcoholics, nail biters, smokers, stutterers, you name it. Every one of them went on to take control over their life simply by changing their perception and mindset. They have proved that it is possible and have inspired me to write this book.

It doesn't matter what the habit is. By definition, it is a pattern of behaviour that becomes difficult to live without. Most of us have experienced how hard it can be to get rid of habits. Let this book work with you in making these changes happen. The chapters are designed to be read in bite-sized chunks so this book is ideal to be read on the go or in a single sitting (for the serious bookworms amongst you).

Remember the key to success is to acknowledge and understand your habit in as much detail as you can. This is the first step to changing your life forever.

This book will allow you to discover the

reasons why we have bad habits, how to determine them, the effects that they bring into our life and, more importantly, how to change and break free.

As you further discover the things you need to do to change your bad habits, make sure to make it a "habit" to read this book as a guide in your journey to change.

ACKNOWLEDGE & ADMIT
THE HABIT

STEP ONE

Acknowledge and Admit the Habit

"Ninety-nine percent of failures come from people who have the habit of making excuses."

George W. Carver

Studies show that almost 40% of the things we do are forms of habit. They are the repetitive patterns or routines that we exercise in our everyday lives. There are good habits and then there are, of course, bad habits! I have had my own share of these - smoking, drinking beer every night (feeling it was the only thing I needed to help me to relax after a tough day at work). I struggled for years to try and break these two but every time I managed just a few weeks, I would celebrate, thinking that I had it mastered and, guess what? Yes! I reward myself with a drink or a cigarette. Sound familiar?

That was before I learnt the true role of the mind for a sustainable lifestyle change. 13 years ago I stopped both overnight (and decided to become a vegetarian at the same time). I have not gone back to that behaviour since. Now I'm certainly not here to tell you to follow my path and give up on drink or anything else you enjoy but the key is not to let the behaviour control us.

Bad habits are negative patterns of behaviour or conduct. They are the things that people repeatedly do, over and over again. However, breaking the pattern of a bad habit can be kind of hard as it has become embedded in daily life at a subconscious level. It may already have become a routine to such an extent that we don't even realise we are doing it. Have you ever had someone point out a habit of yours that you didn't even realise you had? I know I have.

I have been giving public talks for several years. It's almost second nature for me to get up and speak to a crowd of people on a matter that I'm passionate about. I recall several years ago that I was at an event and was suddenly called upon by the host to talk about the power of the mind to an audience of about 200 folk. Now, as you can imagine, this is an area that I'm hugely passionate about and, more often than not, I can ramble on for hours talking on this subject. On this occasion, I got up and gave, what I thought was, an eloquent

20 minute speech on controlling the mind chatter, restructuring our beliefs, setting goals and taking action. The audience was very gracious in its applause and I sat down feeling I might have achieved something that night. I was brought out of my reverie of self-praise, however, with a sharp elbow in the ribs from my then frustrated partner who whispered (rather harshly, I might add) "Why is it that whenever you give a speech you have this stupid habit of wiping your nose with your hand as you are speaking? It looks awful!" Suddenly, it dawned on me that at a movement that I had used as part of my 'speaking style' which I thought portrayed someone who is relaxed had actually morphed into a sub conscious habit that I was completely unaware of. Worse still, it looked like I was wiping my nose with my hand. How awful!

Bad habits come in many forms and a list would be endless. However, here are some common habits we might want to change:

- **Cursing or swearing**: A very common habit that most people do almost every day from all walks of life. Many blame the media and it certainly plays a part, I'm sure. Nowadays, the language used on TV, radio or even newspaper doesn't seem to be regulated as it once was. We are all exposed to bad language, as if it is the norm. Easy access to the internet is another culprit in being exposed to profanities. Not all parents can monitor their children's activities 24/7 thus providing more exposure to bad language. The issue here is that we are all subjected to bad language as if it is the norm and therefore it feels acceptable. This belief of acceptance can give birth to a whole load of habits in the way we communicate. A new online dictionary has been successfully developed just to keep up to date on the emerging street language and swear words (check out www.urbandictionary.com).

- **Nail biting/Picking your nails**: Studies show that most instances of nail biting can be attributed to stress and boredom. Sometimes this shows nervousness or just being uneasy. However, for many, this develops into a much more serious habit. They unconsciously indulge in this behaviour eventually because it has become a sub conscious routine for them. Nail biting or picking your nails can be seen as gross by some but more importantly, it can be very unhealthy (unless you wash your hands 100 times a day or something). It can also cause severe damage to your nails and cuticles because too much biting might lead to irritation and inflammation to the skin that surrounds the nail.

- **Procrastination**: People procrastinate every now and then, but surprisingly around 20% of people constantly avoid doing complicated tasks and intentionally look for some sort of distraction to avoid doing work that is assigned to them. Others, instead of doing things right away, would often choose to delay the task until the deadline is already at hand. In short, they prefer to cram and do things in a hurry. Are you one of these?

This is the habit I am currently working on for myself – a book won't write itself, after all, will it? I have come up strategies to ensure my key tasks get done a regular basis and set myself little goals I can celebrate as a mark of progress now. I will share some of these with you later in the book.

- **Addiction**: There are so many kinds of addiction; from smoking, alcohol, drugs, shopping, eating, gambling and even going to gym – yes you heard right. Ever hear the phrase 'too much of a good thing can be bad for you'. Addictions occur when habits have become so strong that the 'addict' simply feels that they cannot live without a certain kind of habit as a stimulus to feel good. Often addiction can be associated with and triggered by our senses and our experiences. Those things that we smell, see or feel. A familiar place, for example, where you usually do your shopping, even a restaurant with your favourite food or a nearby casino where you can easily access and gamble your heart out.

Very often people associated with your addiction (the ones who are probably addicted themselves) can make it very difficult to break the habit. Remember the age old saying 'You become the company that you keep.' More about this later in the book.

Habits are difficult to change. It's not an overnight process. We all know that they can become destructive to our mind, body and whole well-being. We are not born with these bad habits. They are learned behaviour, influenced by circumstances or people in our lives. This means that they can be unlearnt and replaced by new behaviours. Knowing and admitting that you have them is a good start. It shows that you are determined to make things better for you and that you want to change for the best.

Still not convinced? Rest assured, I have seen client upon client that has had some kind of habit, whether it is behavioural or some kind of habitual pattern of thinking. All of these clients, through coaching to reprogram their thinking behaviour, managed to overcome their habits and transform their lives.

So let's start doing this!

QUICK PLAN

- **Acknowledge that you have a habit in the first place. Admit it to yourself without any sense of trying to justify it.**

- **Tip - Very often, those closest to you recognise your habit quicker than you can.**

KNOW GOOD FROM BAD
IS MY HABIT
HEALTHY?

STEP TWO

Know Good From Bad – Is My Habit Healthy?

"Don't stay in bed, unless you can make money in bed."

George Burns

It is easy to find out if a habit is good or bad. You just need to check the impact on your quality of Life. Quality of life could be defined as the wellness across your daily activities and having optimum health and a great mindset.

It's sensible to suggest, therefore, that good habits, on the other hand, enhance your well-being, improve your relationships and increases the chance of a healthy work environment.

Good vs Bad Habit

Lifestyle plays an important role in gauging your habits. In food preference, if you're into a healthy life style, you will probably prefer eating nutritious food, being aware of the nutritional value of each kind of food that you are eating. Choosing what to eat and reading the labels is a good habit. You focus on how you will benefit from it and you continue to do this to achieve your overall goal.

So when does it become a bad habit? When you become too conscious with what you eat to the point that, if there is no other alternative available at a particular time, you'd rather starve yourself; in this example your good habit could be seen as a bad habit.

Most of our habits affect our daily life and good habits usually help us work easier and faster. Waking early in the morning, eating breakfast before going to work, making sure all our things are organised, doing our assignments and tasks for the day before relaxation are generally considered good habits. They can leave us feeling energised, content and less stressed as a result. They lead to productivity, towards a goal.

These are just some of the things that good habits do to us. In addition, they give us a sense of fulfilment and boosts our self-esteem. If we've been receiving positive feedback and we can see the benefits of the things that we do, then the best thing is to keep that habit – right? We continue doing it because we are able to achieve our goal.

And that's what matters. Continuing the habit will most likely bring out the best in us.

Bad Habits

There are also habits that prevent or slow us from accomplishing our task or goal. Of course, I'm talking about our bad habits. Examples of these vices would include drinking alcohol to the point of dependency, smoking, becoming a couch potato and even oversleeping. Some people may say that some of these habits are just a form of relaxation (or even recreation). In this case gauging whether or not a habit is bad for you depends on how it impacts upon our lives. The question I guess we need to ask ourselves is, 'What effect is it having on my life on a daily basis?'

As already mentioned, good habits improve your quality of life and help you accomplish your task. If doing something regularly prevents you from accomplishing anything or adversely affects your life then clearly it is a bad habit. A good example of this is alcohol addiction. It starts with the social drinks, hanging out with your friends but then you find you're drinking more, sometimes by yourself at home; you find that your behaviour changes, you begin doing or saying things that upset people, you seem to have a constant hangover, you drink more to make you feel good or numb the pain. If you continue along this path there is a good chance you will become addicted in your use of alcohol.

Bad habits are those actions and ways of thinking that have a negative impact on you, your health, your relationships and your progress. You will be able to gauge your habit depending on its effect on you and to others. It is very important to consider all of these to be able to measure the magnitude and severity of damage a habit can have on you. How does your habit affect the way you think, speak or act? If you know that it is not good, it is a bad habit.

KNOW THE IMPACT
CAN HABITS
AFFECT YOUR LIFE?

STEp THREE

Know the Impact – Can Bad Habits Affect Your Life?

"Tell me what you eat, and I will tell you what you are."
Anthelme Brillat-Savarin

Each and every one of us has developed some kind of habit during our life. You can't expect to go through life and not have at least one habit, can you? It could be 'just' something thing that we 'like to do' but we do it often enough for it to become part of our personality.

Whether they are good or bad, the important thing is to be aware of is that habits can affect our lives. Good habits lead you to success in certain aspects of life, where you feel pretty good about yourself and I'm guessing that you already have an idea as to what bad habits can do to you.

The chances are that you are reading this book

because you want to get rid of a bad habit that you know is affecting your life in a negative way. These habits can affect your everyday routine, your performance, productivity, self-esteem, relationships with others and, ultimately, your happiness. Now, you might not be convinced just yet and still be wondering, "How can bad habits ruin my life?" Well, let's have a look at this, shall we?

When It Comes To Work?

Some habits start off as something one might think of as pleasurable. Some are even proud of the habit, it's their trademark.

Meet Paul the Procrastinator. Procrastination is when you tend to delay what you have to do and exchange it with something you'd rather do. That was Paul. He was quite proud that he did things last minute and believed that he actually performed his best work when it was at the last moment. Sound like anyone you know?

Paul did well at work and was popular amongst his colleagues. He let his P.A. keep him organised and prompt him to do the important stuff that needed to be done at the right time. In the meantime, he enjoyed the other more pleasurable tasks. It was fine until Paul decided he wanted to work for himself and start up his own business. He continued with the habit of putting off the more difficult tasks, preferring to cuddle his pillow and stare at his mobile phone, scrolling through social media or watching movies on Netflix. He continued with the mentality that he would perform better last minute and that things could be put off.

The problem was that he didn't have an organised P.A. behind him and, very soon, all of his work started piling up and he began to realise that if he wanted to succeed in his business he needed to get the work done, but by now it had piled up so high it was becoming overwhelming. He started worrying about this and started having sleepless nights until a friend told him something he needed to hear. 'You've got to get yourself organised. If you don't earn the money, nobody else will.'

If you haven't already guessed it, I was Paul!

It took the realisation that my procrastination was now actually preventing my growth and, if not tackled, it would also lead to the failure of my business to kick start myself into action. I have been blessed with some excellent P.A.'s in my previous life as a senior officer in the UK Police Service. Although I've always appreciated them, I only realised their true worth once I no longer had them to prompt me.

I've learned the potential harm that procrastination can do when it comes to work. First is, that you are actually very unproductive in this state. All of the things that matter most are put to the lowest priority and, sooner or later, when things get worse, we tend to cram the work in and all of this leads us to stress and panic, even became depressed. There's no peace when you cram last minute and, rest assured that, even if you've done it on time, chances are it wasn't your best work.

If you are the kind of person who prefers staying up late partying, gaming or watching movies how truly capable are you of delivering excellent performance the next day? By the way, I'm not portraying myself to be some kind of party animal (I would rather leave the partying to others) but movies I absolutely love!

Now, I live life in a much more organised way. It feels great to tick things off the 'To Do' list. I do the most difficult things first, allowing me spend the rest of the day on the more pleasurable work. Hey, I've even realised I can still feed my other habit of watching movies but now I can enjoy them stress-free knowing that my business is going in the right direction.

How Can Bad Habits Ruin Your Relationship?

If you think that your bad habits only affect you, your life and your lifestyle, I'm afraid we only have to look more closely to see that that this couldn't be further from the truth. Bad habits can also, and will surely, affect your relationships with your friends and with your partner.

Bad Habits vs. Friends

When Jackie was at university, she had a bunch of new friends who she just loved hanging out with. She spent her first two years with them. They were such good fun. They loved all the things that she did. They spent a lot of time going to the shopping mall, partying, staying up late at night, talking about their crushes, chatting on social media rather than wasting their time studying. Life was just great! Who would have thought that university would be such fun, hey? They were having a blast. Any of those girls who spent their time being too serious about their studies were simply nerds and weirdos. They weren't fun or cool enough to hang out with. They made it part of their fun to put these girls down at every opportunity.

Some of these girls, like Tracy, were actually Jackie's old school friends but Jackie didn't care about them now because she had new friends to have fun with. I mean, why would she want to

30

hang out with someone who had become such a bore now anyway?

It was fun.

Until Jackie began to fail her exams. Her marks got worse and worse. She got to a point where her professor warned her that she might not make it through to next year as she was unlikely to pass the end of year exams. The horror of this dawned on Jackie. What would her parents say? What kind of future could she possibly have if she failed at university? She began to worry. The dread of this potential nightmare kept her awake at night and fed her fears throughout the day. She found herself going out less and less as she was worrying more about her future. She forced herself to study. The more she studied, the more she started improving her grades and eventually started enjoying the experience.

Her 'girlfriends' soon got so bored of this nerdy Jackie that they started distancing themselves from her. In fact, as she had become so boring, she was game to be put down by the 'cool girls'.

Jackie didn't care though. She had started to mix in different circles with other students who wanted to study, the very same people, like Tracy, that she previously disowned and ridiculed. Soon, she realised her results were picking up again. She was actually starting to pass her exams with flying colours!!

It was then that she realised that her earlier behaviour was simply a form of procrastination. It was more fun to go out with her friends than to spend time studying. It was a distraction from what was more important at this stage of her life.

However, once she started taking responsibility of her life, she enjoyed the gradual improvements. She celebrated every time she passed a test, every time her marks improved. Soon studying became real fun! She passed her final exams and went on to have a great career, following her passion.

I wonder how her old 'friends' did.

I guess the moral of this story is that bad habits can take you away from people that matter most but can influence (and be influenced by) others.

What About Your Partner?

When bad habits turn into vices and addictions they can seriously affect your relationships with those that are closest to you. Don't underestimate this. I mean, there should be a government health warning just on this point, aside from the fact of how it affects your health or other parts of your life. Your bad habits, if left unchecked, can destroy your relationships and hurt those that you care most for.

Nick had it all. I mean he seriously had it all. A great business, a lovely big house and a beautiful family. You can just imagine it.

He always liked a drink, going out with his friends over a weekend and letting go of the stress of the week. Although his business was doing well, it was stressful work. New orders were increasing and Nick was doing everything he could do to meet them. Every day he was coming home tired, he had less time to drink with his friends. He decided he would drink at home instead. It seemed more efficient at the time. However, over the years as business (and pressure) grew, Nick found himself in the habit of picking up beer and a bottle of whisky on the way home most days and he would sit and drink this at home after his meal. Soon his new habit of 'having a drink at home' became so strong that it started dictating his life to an extent. It was much easier to drown himself in his evening drinking binges than to focus on his family or to think about where his business was going. Do you think he was in a fit and productive state each morning when he went to work after these sessions? I suggest not. How do you think it affected his relationships at home?

If his wife ever dared to suggest he was drinking too much he would get angry. How dare she accuse him of being an alcoholic! The thing is Nick *was* becoming that. Deep down he feared it himself but he needed the drink to help him relax after a very busy day.

His wife continued to warn him and he argued more with her. It got to the point that everyone in the family actually avoided him in fear of him getting angry.

Bad Habits vs. Family

Bad habits developed by family members can greatly affect other members since they share the same roof. We can see from Nick's example above how it can affect loved ones.

Let's consider it another way. Say, for example, the father is smoking cigarettes. Since he shares the same house with his children, chances are they get to inhale the smoke from it, right? What could happen then? It might cause them to develop a disease sooner or later.

"Okay, okay!" I hear you shout. "You are just picking up on the obvious habits but that doesn't mean that all habits affect people, does it?" Well let's just consider this. Pick any habit you care to think of and then consider how that habit might be impacting on someone's life along the way. If you look at it closely enough, you will notice that each habit has a direct or indirect impact on someone's life. Whether your habit is having a limiting belief in your own potential, a propensity to anger quickly, eat sugary foods or whatever else, there is an impact on someone. Let's assume that person impacted upon is the person who owns the habit. By the fact that it is now a habit for them it means it will have changed their lifestyle or personality in some way, which could go on to change the way they interact with others thereafter. You see, there are things in this world that we do and often think that it only affects our own lives. We want to continue do things that we think are making us happy but choosing not to believe the effect it has on others in our life.

You might just have one of these bad habits right now in your life; but you know what? You still have time to change it. It might not be immediate but, sooner or later, you'll see that it's worth it. Not only that it would result in better opportunities in life but it can also improve your relationships with others in your life.

QUICK PLAN

- **Be very clear of the area(s) of your life that are affected by your habit.**

- **What would happen if you continued with this habit?**

KNOW THE IMPACT
HEALTH & WEALTH

STEP FOUR

Know the Impact – Health and Wealth

"It is health that is real wealth"
Mahatma Gandhi

Okay so we've looked at how habits can affect our lives and that should be reason enough to chuck them in and get on with a new life, healthy in its widest sense.

However, if you still need convincing, let's just look at how it hits you in you in your health and in your pocket. Now, I'm not saying that all habits will affect your health or your finances (although guaranteed there will be wider impact on your life as we discussed in the previous chapter.)

Let's focus on the two 'biggies' that we all recognise – smoking and alcohol.

Smoking

So we all know that smoking is bad for us,

right? You increase your chances of lung cancer, it makes your clothes smell, you become breathless more easily but did you know that it also affects you in the following ways?

- Smoking reduces oxygen to your skin ageing you far more quickly than a non-smoker.
- You increase your chances of getting mouth, throat, as well as lung cancer.
- You are much more likely to get gum disease.
- It clogs the arteries in your heart and is one of the major factors in strokes and heart disease.
- You increase the chances of infertility and miscarriages.
- It can cause impotence.

Before you get yourself all depressed reading this list though, it is important to understand it is also never too late to stop smoking and dramatically improve your health at any age. The human body is an amazing thing and has a way of repairing itself. After ten years, the risk falls to the same level as someone who never smoked. How cool is that then?

It's not just your heart that improves. Stop smoking and lung capacity could improve by up to 10% within nine months. Imagine what it can do after 9 years!

If that's not enough, your sex life can reach new heights. Improved circulation can lead to bigger erections for men (that should mean something for you fellas) and the woman is likely to have more powerful orgasms.

I'm sold and I don't even smoke anymore!

If you still need convincing let's look at how hard smoking hits your pockets. I have calculated this in both British Sterling and US Dollars currency but the costs will be pretty similar wherever you are in the world, based on someone smoking 20 cigarettes a day. The table below comes from the National Health Service in the UK. Check out what you are spending and what you could spend it on instead:

Time	Savings	
After one month	£183 ($285 USD)	If you stopped smoking, after a month you could afford to take a special weekend break or buy an

		iPod. Your skin would begin to look clearer, brighter and younger as well.
After six months	£1,095 ($1,705 USD)	After six months, the savings would start mounting up. The money you would have saved could be turned into a round-the-world ticket or a luxury cruise. By now your clothes and home would be smelling fresher too.
After one year	£2,190 ($3,411 USD)	After a year, if you've saved all you would have spent on smoking, you'd have a nest egg equivalent worth more than one month's average pay in the

		UK. Think what you could do with all that extra money. You would also suffer fewer coughs and colds.
After five years	£10,950 ($17,060 USD)	After five years, your savings would have really totted up – we are talking about more than one year's average UK mortgage repayments. Imagine paying off your mortgage one year early. Your risk of a heart attack would also have fallen significantly.
After ten years	£21,900 ($34,119 USD)	After ten years, you would have saved more than the equivalent of two years' mortgage

		repayments. Imagine paying off your mortgage two years early.

Alcohol

Again, we are told that excessive drinking of alcohol can affect our health but what exactly can it do to us? According to the UK NHS, compared to non-drinkers, if you regularly drink above higher-risk levels:

- You could be 3-5 times more likely to get cancer of the mouth, neck and throat.
- You could be 3-10 times more likely to develop liver cirrhosis.
- Men could have four times the risk of having high blood pressure, and women are at least twice as likely to develop it.
- You could be twice as likely to have an irregular heartbeat.
- Women are around 1.5 times as likely to get breast cancer.

It is important to remember that most people who have alcohol-related health problems aren't necessarily alcoholics but simply have drunk regularly more than the recommended levels for some years. Binge drinking doesn't make you any less vulnerable to disease. Massive over consumption in a short time frame can also lead to alcohol poisoning.

Macmillan Cancer Support in the UK reported that each Briton spends around £787 a year on alcohol, with London's concentration of drinkers spending sizably more. The research, conducted by Onepoll, surveyed 2,000 over-18s. Men spent an average of £934.44 ($1455.81 USD) per year, the data found, compared with women spending £678.60 ($1,057.22 USD). This is about £50,000 ($77,897.50 USD) in their life time!! Staggering figure, isn't it? Particularly when you consider that the average wage in UK is £26,000 ($40,506.70 USD)! That means that most of us are spending 2 years of our hard-earned cash on drink during our life time. What could you do with that extra money? How could it change your life?

The drinking culture is a global affair. The average USA citizen spends $1 USD in every $100 on alcohol.

Responsible drinking of alcohol through a change in your drinking habits and routines can have huge impact on the health and the pocket.

Whilst we have focused on alcohol and

smoking, it's very important that we realise that everything we consume has an impact on our bodies (and of course our finances).

Even the lesser-known habits that we perhaps don't even think about. Those that seem harmless on the face of it.

Whilst tea and coffee have some health properties, some studies have shown that excessive drinking can lead to tremors, anxiety and insomnia, not to mention the addictive effects of caffeine. Coffee shop chains are pretty much universal now and offer a fantastic range of flavours but consider the calories and size of the cup before you buy. Most will do a skimmed milk version of a lot of their coffees.

Even the common nail biters should give some serious thought to the implications of their habits. Nail biting can result in:

1. Transferring disease-causing bacteria into your mouth
2. Warts in your mouth from any infections you may have on your hands
3. An infection called paronychia, where bacteria enter through damaged skin. This can require surgical treatment to drain it off in serious cases

4. Constant nail biting can misshapen your teeth and affect the natural closing of the jaw where the upper and lower teeth meet.

For more information, here are just some of the useful websites I have found.

- **www.nhs.uk/livewell**
- **http://www.nlm.nih.gov/medlineplus/ magazine/issues/spring07/articles/spring 07pg14-17.html**
- **https://www.lifeline.org.au/Get-Help/Facts---Information/Substance-Abuse---Addiction/Substance-Abuse-and-Addiction**
- **http://www.lung.org/stop-smoking**
- **http://www.howtogiveupsmoking.co.uk/**
- **http://www.smokenders.com.au/**

QUICK PLAN

- Specifically test to see how your habit affects your health or wealth.

- What would happen if you continued with this habit?

STOP MAKING EXCUSES!

STEP FIVE

Stop Making Excuses!

"They say that nobody is perfect, then they say that practice makes perfect. I wish they'd make up their minds."

Unknown

N obody is perfect." How many times have you heard this? It's true, nobody really is perfect, but this shouldn't be an excuse for not trying to improve, should it?

In this section we are going to ponder on why people make excuses, why it can be obstacle to moving forward, and how to take action against it and help you smash that bad habit.

The Rational Excuse

What does this actually mean? Well in this context it is about making up some seemingly plausible or logical excuse for not correcting our mistakes or overcoming failures. It's all too easy to become defensive about our mistakes and end up in some state of denial about it. Our bad habits may bring us shame and we may not want to be reminded of that. This is exactly one of reasons why we hide behind excuses instead of confronting them. We all do it, to a lesser or greater extent. The thing is that, no matter how you hide that habit, it will be revealed sooner or later.

Now, ask yourself, do you want to get rid of those bad habits? Or are you willing to take the risk of continuing them?

If you want to break the chains that keep you from doing what's right, take the first step. Acknowledge and admit it. Acknowledging that bad action means that you are now ready to take the next big steps of change and it is a way of showing that you are willing to turn away from it starting at this moment.

Break Your Rationalising Beliefs

It is never easy. Leaving the things you are so used to doing and replace them with others that will make you a different person. Most people don't like change or are, at least, uncomfortable with the process of it. There are some thoughts, that some of us have, which prevent us from embracing change. These thoughts are our *beliefs*. We all have belief systems that we have accumulated throughout our lives through the people and things we have experienced. Some of these beliefs prevent us from changing and improving our lives. There are so many examples of these 'beliefs' but here are just some examples of how they manifest themselves in your thinking:

Negativity

Let's be quite frank here. Can you truly say, hand-on-heart, that all of life is bad? Of course you can't. Even the most disillusioned of us can think of a moment in their lives that made them smile. Not all of life is bad so stop moping around and pretending that it is. The more you think in a negative language, the more you will notice negative events and experiences which simply reinforce your belief that everything is bad.

Life is perfectly in balance; where there is bad there is also good. Sometimes the bad experiences are there simply to help you appreciate the good when you see it. However, if you are not looking for the good, chances are you won't even notice it - even when it is under your nose. This will not help you. The first thing we have to do to break these limiting beliefs is to see ourselves differently. Have some faith in ourselves and believe that it is entirely possible for us to change our habits. Smash through those excuses and believe that you can potentially do anything if you want to!

Encourage yourself! Stop being a pessimist. Don't let that negative vibe pull you down and allow it to consume you. Everyone wants to be a winner, right? You don't want to let that attitude kill you, do you? Then think positive! Remember: **you can do it**!

Afraid of What Other People Might Think

Ever heard of the phrase 'peer group pressure'? Most kids will have because it's more acute at their young impressionable age. Social media has extended our circle of friends and associates further than we have ever known. Many people are frightened of doing something different because of what their ever-growing circle of friends, their families or the community might think. Well, here's the thing. If what you are trying to do is a positive thing aimed at improving your heath, relationships and general happiness you really have to question how much these people, who are the naysayers in your life, really care about you. Perhaps it is time to start weeding out your social group or distancing yourself from those who will prevent you from progressing.

Choose Your Company Carefully

What do you think would happen if you kept the company of thieves, or drug users, alcoholics, people who swear constantly? You would have a greater chance of becoming a thief, a drug user, start drinking heavily or being abusive. It stands to reason that you are likely to emulate those whose company you are in all the time. Remember Jackie from our earlier story? She got into a crowd who preferred shopping over studying. It was only a matter of time before her studies suffered.

Distance yourself from people who might influence you into bad habits. One of the reasons why you have your habit is perhaps because you were surrounded by people who also had it.

Now what is the solution? Simple, choose your peer group carefully. If your companions have the same habit as that you are trying to rid yourself of then it will become extremely difficult, if not impossible, for you to change. They are hardly likely to be able to give you the moral encouragement you need, after all, are they? The only exception to this is if they are also on the same mission as you, in which case, they may be the best people to align yourself with as you have a shared experience.

This doesn't mean that you will *lose* all your friends; it does mean, however, you must *choose* your friends. Know what company you should have. A true friend will always want the best for you. So, if you have a friend that would provoke you to do something that you know is not good for you, he or she is not a true friend and you should consider walking away from their constant company.

Take Action

Nothing can be achieved without action! It's not enough that you have learned how to destroy limiting beliefs or that you are clear of your goal. You must translate all of that good work in to action.

If you buy medicine to cure a disease but don't actually take it, do you think it will make you better? The disease is still there and it might just get worse. The infection will continue to destroy you. How about when you have an exam coming up and you have all the text books. Do you think that walking around with the books without ever reading them is going to increase your knowledge? That, by some chemical reaction, the information contained within the books is going to be absorbed by your skin and into your brain? Of course not.

Why, therefore, would you expect to achieve any change in your life without taking action? Here are a few things you can start practicing as you begin to turn your back on a habit:

Ignore

I know, I know, like I've said, it is not that easy but if you are determined enough to let go and win over that situation, then ignore! Ignore what? Ignore the feeling of wanting to go back. Sometimes those feelings will be the reasons for you to fall again but you can let it get to you. These feelings are only temporary and your body's way of telling you it is feeling outside of its comfort zone but, remember, that is where true growth is.

Don't Give Up

Just keep on trying! You are halfway there, my friend. Do not give up and do **not** look back!

Think Find and Hone a Talent

Why not play and practice your favourite instrument. Maybe take up golf, gardening, painting or whatever. Who knows where that hobby may lead you, right? It's all about finding an alternate distraction that you enjoy.

There are so many hobbies out there to

choose from. The list is truly endless. My advice is that you pick something that you've always wanted to do or are interested in. Make a list of all of the things and start working down them. Guaranteed that for every interest, there will be a group you can join, a product you can get hold of. Google is an amazing tool, right? Another useful website you can check is www.meetup.com.

Self-Pity Is Wasted Pity

Never pity yourself. I mean, what does it actually achieve? Pitying yourself means you are admitting how weak you are, and you are not! Stop thinking thoughts that might cause you to sit down in the corner and condemn yourself forever just because you have finally stopped the bad habit that you were in to.

If I could only count the number of clients that have come to me with the deep-seated thought of being the victim in life or a failure and that others should feel sorry for them. They feel wrong done by the world. 'Why me?' is a phrase too often thrown about with abandonment.

Here's the thing. You might get people feeling sorry for you initially but when they repeatedly hear you bemoaning your life do you really think they will continue to pity you? Think about it, would you?

One only has to look through the timelines of their Facebook accounts to see friends moaning about something or another and they seem to be the same people, time and time again. Why is that? If you go through life with the attitude that everything is bad, that bad things only happen to you then, guess what? You are probably right, because you are attracting them into your life through your thoughts and subtle actions.

Me? I keep my timeline very clear of negativity. Bringing my energy levels up to a peak state most of the time is a result of a lot of hard work on my part. Why let the negative energy of others bring them down? Sure, we all have bad days and good days and I'm not saying you should be happy-clappy all the time (or sooner or later someone might get really worried about you).

I focus on getting my clients into a positive mindset before we tackle their underlying issue. It is critically important for your success and I encourage you to see life in a much more different way too as you embark this journey of transformation.

Stop being bitter and start being better! Believe in yourself. It works, I promise!

Be Grateful

Ever heard of the attitude of gratitude? I live my life by it. It's worth remembering that our lives are full of experiences that, if we were to stop and think about them, we could be truly grateful for. From the roof over our heads, the food on our table, through to the people in our lives. It is very easy to take all of this for granted, don't you think? No matter how big we think our current problem is, we can always find someone else who has it much, much harder than us.

Every time you think you've had a bad day try this experiment. Sit down for just half an hour at the end of day. Find somewhere quiet, where there are no distractions. Somewhere you can think. Now, go through your day from start to finish in as much details as you can and jot down on a piece of paper all those things that were actually positive. Remember to look out for those things that we have started taking for granted so much that they have become invisible to us. I'm talking about the smallest things like your first coffee of the day, the warm water in the shower, the smell of the soap, the first smile you saw. And so on – you get the picture? As you remember each thing write it down on your piece of paper.

Once you have your list (and we need to be

aiming for at least 20 on our first go – don't worry, they are definitely there) read your list out to yourself. Slowly.

How does it make you feel?

You could choose to be grateful because you've finally decided to smash this habit out of your life. That has got to be something worth feeling good about, don't you think? You've started a new lease of life. You have every excuse to feel good about taking action on this.

Good or bad, you should always be thankful! The more grateful you are, the more you will notice to be even more grateful about.

Learn

There is always something to learn, remember that. Your past experiences do not define the person you are today; it is how you respond to them that really matters. As they say "the past is the past" and it is best left where it belongs – behind you.

If you were driving your car looking backwards all the time, what do you think could happen? Yes. You are likely to crash! Similarly, living in the past either won't get you to your desired destination because you are at risk of crashing and failing. Take every step as a new lesson to learn and not a burden to bear.

Yes, it is challenging to change your normal routines but remember that, once you step outside of that comfort zone you are into what I call the 'growth zone'. You will learn new ways of thinking, new ways of doing things that you had perhaps never even considered before. The more you try new stuff the more you learn. The more you learn the more you grow.

Everything starts with the thoughts that you are willing to allow to occupy the precious space inside your mind. Keep them strong and positive. Get rid of negativity and bad company and do not listen to the naysayers. Learn from the challenges that occur in life rather than ask yourself how you could improve the next time. Once you have mastered this, you are totally going to grow.

This isn't going to happen overnight. It will take time, patience and most of all... practice.

QUICK PLAN

- Note down the reasons why you feel you *want* to smash this habit.

- Pin them up for you to see every day and serve to remind you.

- You might also want to think about what your hobby/interest you might want to take up that will serve as a positive distraction.

START SMALL
FINISH BIG

STEP SIX

Start Small, Finish Big

"The great pleasure in life is doing
what people say you cannot do."
Walter Bagehot

Everyone fails. In this multi-faceted existence called LIFE, it stands to reason that you've already had your fair share of failure as well as success; I know I have. Your failures may even be habitual, such as making bad decisions, taking miscalculated risks, and embracing incorrect or limiting beliefs (like telling yourself you are not worthy of success and so on). Whatever the reason we may have, the fact is that we have all failed at something at some point in our lives and there is nothing we can do to change it.

This quote from the hugely inspirational J. K. Rowling, better known as the creator of the Harry Potter books, sums it up nicely.

It is impossible to live without failing at something, unless you live so cautiously that you might as well not have lived at all, in which case you have failed by default.

J. K. Rowling

Hang on a minute though - that does not mean you can't start over again, right? Well, you can and you will! With the additional benefit of learning from experience.

So how do I get started?

We can all be impatient. It is natural to want everything instantly – the big house, fancy car, great life and a thriving career. If you were Aladdin then you could consider this problem sorted. However, we don't all have a genie. Rome was not built in a day (or even a couple of months, come to that).

Wanting so much at once and being impatient to see the results often leads to frustration, disappointment and more failure until it becomes a vicious cycle. Unless you change the way you see things and the future. Remember these simple thoughts:

- To climb a mountain you need to start from

63

the bottom
- Every journey starts with the first step
- Experts weren't born overnight, they were also novices once
- Every master was once a disaster

You can start building your small blocks of victories by learning to take the small steps. Taking the **baby steps to success** may sound simple to do, but it requires dedication and understanding of the advantages of creating a cycle of small victories.

1. **Start with a SMART action plan rather than just any kind of plan**.
Your goal must be:

S - Specific
M - Measurable
A - Attainable
R - Realistic
T - Timebound

Be clear about what you are trying to achieve. What is your goal? What does it look like? How will you measure your progress towards this goal?

This section will give you some pointers on this but you may have other ideas to make sure that you are staying true to your path.

Whatever your goal is, it has to attainable. This goes hand in hand with it being realistic. What point is there in striving for something that is not achievable? How realistic would it that be?

Finally, give yourself a timescale to achieve your goal. If you know anything about project management, you would know that one the first things that has to be made commonly clear is the goal. Thereafter, you would develop a series of milestones or smaller goals that will eventually take you to your final destination. Each of these would have timescales to keep you on track for a delivery date. It's no different with life changes.

Make sure you put in a time limit and milestones to check on your progress. You might start with a week at first, perhaps moving on to two weeks or a month of being habit free. Whatever milestones you set, make sure that you celebrate each one as you achieve. It is a massive achievement, after all. Think of how you might want to reward yourself now. Don't expect too much of yourself. Be realistic. You are not going to shed 5 stone in a month or become Arnold Schwartznegger overnight when you've been a couch potato for the last five years but you could become noticeably stronger in the space of a month with regular exercise and a healthy diet. Be clear about what you want to achieve, by what date and don't plan for failure by making it too unrealistic to begin with.

2. **Take Action.**

Your ambition will not take you anywhere if you do not take action. Kickstart yourself by being clear on what the first few steps might be. This way you will build up momentum to keep up with the rest of your plan. The initial steps really need to be clear and well thought through but not overly complicated. For example, if your goal is to lose fat, you could start by keeping a diary of your eating habits to understand where the loopholes are. This only takes moments. A journal is a great way of monitoring yourself on your habits.

3. **Check your progress and keep moving forward.**

This is your opportunity to check the results of your progress. Pay close attention to yourself. Be aware of when you are performing your bad habits most during the day. What are the triggers? How can you change your daily routine to replace them with new triggers? If you like to smoke after every meal, what alternatives could you choose? I took to drinking a glass of ice cold water instead and really savoured it. It worked for me. You can develop a schedule for workouts. Start by 10 or 20 minutes per day, and increase it when you have got the hang of it. Again, do not torture yourself with the idea of INSTANT SUCCESS.

4. **Repeat steps #02 and #03 until you start building a habit.**

Assess your development at the end of every week. If you are able to shed about 2-4 lbs per week simple maths will tell us that you could eliminate 48 lbs in 6 months. How incredible does that sound? Hold on to your goal until you find yourself moving more naturally. It's simply a case of overcoming the inertia until you gain momentum.

Those mini-victories, are your milestones and checkpoints to ensure that you are moving forward. If you want it enough bad enough you **can** achieve it. Milestones (or these little steps) will ensure that you are heading in the right direction. You will be able to 'power through' your pain and past failures. On top of these, you will also gain a whole new perspective about success.

Think of this as a long distance race not a sprint.

QUICK PLAN

- **Write down your SMART action plan. How will you check your progress to know that you are going in the right direction?**

- **#Tip - Using a calendar to set milestones dates so they are visible might be very useful.**

STEP SEVEN

Pair Up Habits – Kill Two Birds With One Stone

"Let him who would enjoy a good future waste none of his present."

Roger Babson

Most bad habits actually manifest in at least pairs. That is to say, one bad habit is either resulting in another or results from another.

'Have you gone mad?' I hear you yell. 'Habits don't give birth.' Well, let's just think about this. Think about this story and see if you can identify the pairings of habits.

Sarah the Shopaholic

Sarah was just your regular girl. She had a bunch of girlfriends, her own apartment and a decent job in a nearby law firm. Her problem was that she didn't seem to be able to make friends at work.

Everyone there was much older than her, had families and she had nothing in common with them. All they ever seemed to talk about was their kids, husbands or wives, domestic chores, etc. You get the picture.

Poor Sarah, her interests lay in shopping for the latest tops or shoes; after all she was young. She would come back home to an empty apartment, having hardly spoken to anyone at work all day.

Her only enjoyment came when she met her girlfriends and they went shopping. To overcome her unhappiness she would buy her favourite garments and shoes. It made her feel so good that she even started stopping off at the mall sometimes on her way home just to feel the buzz after a lonely day at work. She could afford it, couldn't she? She had a job and a credit card. She would pay it off at the end of every month.

However after a couple of months of spending heavily on the credit card she started to find that her monthly bills were getting higher and higher, to the point that all her money went on paying off her bills and she couldn't afford to go out with her girlfriends.

She started to worry about her situation. She started to have sleepless nights worrying about how she was going to pay off her cards. She hardly saw her friends. She was now lonely at work and at home.

She started researching options and found that her credit score was still quite healthy so she got another card to transfer her balance interest free. Phew! Now she had some breathing space. To celebrate, she went shopping. She deserved it!

What do you think happened to Sarah? Chances are she also maxed out the second card and ended up even more miserable. What two key habits do you think were paired up here?

Sarah was fed up at work and loved shopping. It was her hobby but soon became out of control because she was doing it for the wrong reasons, to fill a gap in her state of mind. Her habitual shopping led to her overspending on her credit card. However, when she got another card, she become so dependent on spending on credit that she went and shopped even more leading to a vicious cycle of debt.

This is just one example of how habits can align themselves. Others could include:

1. Procrastination - Dodging the Gym

I know I've been guilty of this in the past. When you are a procrastinator, you may have all the best intentions. You just make up excuses to put them off. Why? Because taking action can be hard, of course!

We all know that going to the gym, especially after a long time, is not easy. It hurts at first and many of us give up pretty soon because of the pain (if you don't believe me just compare how full the gyms are every January and then check again in February). We start to make excuses to ourselves that we need to do certain 'very important' chores before we go to the gym and take our time. By the time those chores are complete we tell ourselves it's too late to go today but we will go tomorrow. Sound familiar?

So here we have procrastinating behaviour being played in one of its most common ways, the gym. If were to recognise this we might take a no-nonsense approach that the gym is a must and stick to the routine. This could lead you to make schedules for other areas of your life and, 'Hey Presto!' You are not such a big procrastinator as you once were.

2. Stressing – Eating Comfort Foods

This one is another common example. In everyday life, we encounter issues that are challenging.   We feel stressed about our friends, families, or our work colleagues (as Sarah was.) We feel stressed over break-ups, we stress ourselves out because of bills to pay, our credit cards, the list becomes endless. Sometimes it's just easier to sit at home and just drown our sorrows in so-called 'comfort foods'.

The problem is that most comfort foods aren't that healthy. I'm guessing that any person who could create a healthy comfort food might find themselves very wealthy.

Eating ice cream, cake, chocolate when you are broken hearted, eating different kinds of sweets when feeling down or stressed. After all, when the word 'stressed' is spelled out in reverse, it shouts out "desserts" – a good anagram, but definitely not a healthy practice to follow.

Eating comfort foods actually urges you to spend more, become overweight, unhealthy and leads to even more stress (don't sound so comfortable now, do they?)

Instead of finding relief in your comfort foods, why not deal with stress head on? Confront the core of the issues that are bothering you. Identify what actions to take in order to address the things that cause your stresses.

3. Excessive Online Gaming – Staying up Late at Night

Are you addicted to online games? Do you find yourself saying to yourself, 'Just one more game and then I'll go to bed?' If the answer is yes, then perhaps, you can relate to this: online gaming is fun but not the most productive of hobbies. It's designed to provide entertainment but should it control your life to the extent that you want to do little else but play until the wee hours of the night?

Constant deprivation of sleep can actually lead to an immune system breakdown making you more susceptible to viruses leading to disease and ill-health. Limit your exposure time. If you play 10 hours straight why not reduce it to 5 hours a day. I know it might sound difficult or too drastic but, why not try to wean yourself off gaming by gradually reducing the time spent in front of the gaming console or mobile phone? This will lead to less late nights, better sleep and, most likely, more energy throughout the day. Who knows, you might even become a better player.

Understanding the emergence of bad habit pairs

To manage your bad habits will require some strong decision-making but I guess if you've come this far into the book you are willing to do just that.

Before you can manage smashing them all, once and for all, it's important that you first commit. This will affect your decisions on the 'how' during the process of change.

I'm not saying this will be an easy journey but it will most definitely be worth it. It might be tough to maintain the initial momentum but don't let procrastination kick in causing you to fall back into age old habits.

Say you skip your exercise – doing it once can be forgiven but not doing it again and again to the extent that you get used to not doing it. You will eventually find yourself caught under the spell of frequently dodging your routine, eventually leading to the development of the habit of PROCRASTINATION.

The long term effect? It's you, fattening yourself out in front of the TV and eventually affecting your health and lifestyle (see earlier steps).

Just imagine how far the simple skipping of exercise can go.

Bad Habit Pairs and Their Countermeasures

The principle behind a successful method of breaking bad habits is quite simple – do it in pairs. The idea is this: if you indulge yourself with your first bad habit, make sure that the second bad habit is sacrificed as a means to balance out your first.

For instance, let's say you laze around on the couch watching your favourite TV shows instead of going for a walk for exercise. This becomes your first bad habit. The secondary bad habits that can develop along with watching TV is for you to eat junk foods, drink soda, and eat chocolate and other food stuff – these should be given up. This also means that if you tackle the primary habit of watching TV there is a good chance you would also have a lesser desire or opportunity to eat junk food.

The solution, therefore is to recognise bad habit pairs and recognise that if you are going to tackle the main habit, find a way to tackle the associated habit as well. It will actually ease your transformation. Plus you will have killed two birds with one stone!

Go for it!!

QUICK PLAN

- **Look closer at your habit and consider what other negative behaviour comes from this habit. Just think, by tackling one habit you might actually smash two – how cool is that?**

WANT IT REALLY BADLY!

STEP EIGHT

Want it Really Badly

"The difference between a successful person and others is not a lack of strength, not a lack of knowledge, but rather a lack of will."

Vince Lombardi

Okay! So now that you know what your habits are, sorted them into good and bad, know the impact they can have on your life, drawn up a schedule for defeating the habit, you can now start asking yourself do I really want this? Do I really *want* to stop get this habit out of my life? Think about what drives people to change? Where does this desire come from?

Wanting to Stop the Bad Habit Because of the Bad Effects

When trying to break a habit it's natural, no it's necessary, to ask yourself why you want to break away from it. We know now that the answer is pretty straightforward in most cases. The habits are affecting our health, relationships, work or lifestyle and we need to free ourselves of this addictive behaviour in order to transform our lives. Sometimes we simply would be better off to not have this habit in our lives anymore. We want to change our life in some way. It can be that we decide to change our lifestyle or habit because of some other life experience (I remember buying a brand new set of golf clubs after getting divorced once and I've never yet set foot inside a golf club, let alone go onto the course itself).

There can be many reasons to break your habit, but does it give you a strong enough desire to stop or (like my golfing dream) is it just going to be a temporary whim? It's important that you have a very frank discussion with yourself before you make a start on anything. Why? Just because you feel you want to rid yourself of a habit is not always a strong enough driver in order to maintain a sustained change to your lifestyle. You need to really desire it, you need to *want* it from your very soul and have that mission that you want to improve your life by smashing that habit.

If you think about it, you can just as easily rationalise in your mind that maybe the habit doesn't or won't affect your life adversely or that it's pointless worrying about its bad effects because they are so very far into the future. What I mean to say is that if your sole reason for stopping is this reason, you might need more. A deeper seated desire to really transform your life in this aspect is needed.

There are several ways to rationalise why you might want to change a habit. Here are just some of the reasons you might use:

Stop Bad Habits by Desiring to be a Better Person

A great way to drive yourself to stop bad habits is quite simply to desire to be a better person in another aspect of your life. Think about it, if you lose the habit you can only better yourself, can't you? Choose a goal that you want to achieve in another area of your life. Consider how the habit is a blockage to achieving success in that area. Imagine if that habit wasn't there. How more achievable would your goal be?

Desire to Influence Others

This should also rank high in your desire to change. You should *want* to set a new standard that will influence others. Maybe it's others who have bad habits like yours. You have the ability to influence them to transform their own lives. However, in order for you to do that, you must start with yourself.

Have you ever been inspired by friends, family, colleagues who seem to achieve amazing transformations with quiet determination? You know, the person who sheds a few stones in weight in just a few months, the one who runs a marathon six months after only just learning to run at all, someone who overcomes their fear of heights by jumping out of a plane. Remember how you felt inside when you saw their success? There may well have been a hint of envy in there but I'm sure that you were also very impressed by their achievements, even if it was reluctant (and depending on how much you liked them in the first place).

Can you also recall that, once this person had announced their achievement, others around them also started trying to change their lives in some small way? Never underestimate the power we have to influence change in others.

Prove to them that anything is achievable in life. Be the hero!

How to Find the Willpower to Succeed

Now that you have established *why* you want to smash your habit, you need the will power to bring it to life. The real question is not really the *how* to find the willpower to break your bad habits but more about *where* to find it. So let's look at some possible places where you might find that willpower.

Find it in your family and loved ones

Close your eyes for a moment and think about the person or people who are the most important in your life right now. Think about them very hard. Have you noticed that, when you think of someone or something very hard, your mind presents you with a cinematic image of them or it?

Okay now, imagine the bad habit you want to erase or change. If, for example, it is alcohol think of all the bad effects it has on your life now and can cause you in the long term. Think about the chances of getting liver cancer or any of the other diseases we looked at earlier associated with alcohol abuse. Now, consider how any future ill health resulting from your habit might impact on the people that you care about. Think about the things that might befall them should you become ill. Now, what do you want to do?

Thinking about the effects your habit is having on others is a sobering reminder of the reality of why you want to stop it now.

Find it in your circle of friends

They say true friends are there for you in good times and bad. Consider your current circle of friends. Who is the closest one to you? Talk through your plans with them. Tell him or her about the things you desire, about how much you want to change and be a better person. Enlist this friend to support you and coach you. Listen to that person and gather that extra willpower from him or her.

It's important that this person is there to help you and guide you on your journey. He or she is not going to push you off that cliff but rather be your parachute. Never underestimate the power of a coach who can support you through your transformation.

Find it in yourself

This is the most important and best place to find that much needed willpower. If you can't find it within you, it becomes a tougher journey because you are constantly battling against yourself.

Think of your inner potential; search for it in the

depths of your mind. Trust me, you have got it. We all have vast untapped resources of inner potential to achieve much more than we could ever believe of ourselves. The limits that we set ourselves are just the limits of our own thinking. If we were to change our perspective by just a tiny bit it can make a huge difference to our future achievements. Consider it this way. If a ship's captain were to alter the course off by just one degree, do you think that ship would still reach it's destination port which is 1000 kilometers away? The problem is that we are so busy allowing our minds to run around like a wild animal that it becomes very difficult to focus on the most important issue. The mind has a tendency to reflect on all of those things that are bothering us (at this instance you are probably thinking about your habit again). We find it difficult to look deep inside ourselves and find that huge untapped power source within us. It is there just waiting for you to use it.

Meditation is my favourite way to allow my mind to rest and let the power within me rise. Now there are various forms of meditation out there. It has almost become too complicated but let's just try something very simple.

Meditation that we can practise every morning

for only ten minutes or so. Whilst, I've been meditating for years, this particular one just helps to set my mental state for the day.

So every morning, commit to spending just ten minutes of this meditation before you go and do anything else. You might want to put on some soothing meditation music (you can buy these for as little as 99p from Amazon).

Okay, so just find yourself sitting in a very comfortable position and breathe…

As you breathe, just imagine that your body is filling with an energy…

Allow that energy to travel down your body from the top of your head – just like the water flows down your body when you have a nice warm shower…

Allow the energy to flow down to every part of your body, to the tips of your fingers and toes…

Every time you feel it going down your body allow that part to relax and loosen…

It might help if you feel your body, relaxing deeper with every exhale…

Repeat this three times

Now whilst in that relaxed state, think of three things (one at a time) that you are grateful for in your life. These can be anything or anyone. Allow your gratitude for them to spread and you might find yourself begining to smile.

Again, repeat three times, once for each person or thing.

Finally, imagine 3 things that you want to achieve in the future, perhaps in 5 or 10 years' time. Maybe it's a vibrant, happy lifestyle, free of your habit, stronger or more secure relationships, promotion in your work or success in your business. It really doesn't matter so long as it is what you want. Now, project yourself into the future and imagine you already having that thing, that lifestyle or that you are in that relationship. Imagine it as if you are already there and note how you are feeling whilst you are there. Are you happy in this place in 5 years time? Are you stronger, richer and freer? Feel it and let that feeling gently flow through your body.

Enjoy this feeling for a few minutes before you gently open your eyes and then go conquer that habit, go conquer that day and master your life!

FOCUS ON YOUR FUTURE

Think of the Things You Want to Do

They say that we only live once, so surely you have a bucket list of the things you want to do. If you do not have one yet, why not give it a try and go create one for yourself.

Focus on the things you still want to do, of the adventures you want to go on in the future. Maybe it is scuba diving, sky diving, skiing, going on a road trip, or maybe it's just going somewhere you have not been to for a long time. What really matters is that there is something that hooks you into wanting that future goal. If you really want to achieve them, we have to prioritise and get rid of the habits that might prevent us from achieving our goal.

Think of the Things You Want to Have

If you had all the money in the world right about now, what would you buy? Why? Now, that's a question that could take you a long time to answer completely. My experience is that when you don't have a clear vision, it's very easy to end up changing your mind on a day by day basis. If you don't have a clear idea and passion for where you want to get to, it's very easy to become distracted by other 'stuff' in our lives, such as our habits. Think of it this way, if you have a well paying job right now and you are able to save some of your earnings, eventually, you will be able to buy the things that you really want. However, if your habit interferes to such an extent that your job security is at risk, you might never be able to buy the dream house, car, holiday or whatever else. You have to really ask yourself, "Is my habit important for me?" or simply, "Is my habit serving my best interests?" The answer should be an easy, "no" to both. By asking yourself these simple but powerful questions, you will be able to decide what remains and what goes out from your life. In simple terms, it's just about 'doing right by yourself'.

Think of your future with someone special

A great way to motivate you to stop and break that bad habit is to think of that someone special and your future together. Imagine your special someone; imagine the shade of his or her hair, the colour of his or her eyes. Imagine them in as much detail as you can. I am sure you have memorised them. I am sure that as you are reading this, you can perfectly imagine their face in your mind's eye.

Now, I want you to look at what would happen to you 10 years from now. What do you see now? Do you see yourself married or living in a beautiful house with kids? Maybe you are travelling together and enjoying discovering new places and people.

Imagine what your life *could* look like in those 10 years if you were to continue your bad habit.

How could it affect your relationship with someone special? It's important to be honest and stark with yourself in this visualisation. How has your relationship been affected? Look at the image in your mind in as much detail, colour and sound as you can.

Now take a breath, shake out your arms and legs and try something different. Imagine that you have smashed the habit and project yourself into the future once more. Do you see a different picture now? A more happy, successful picture maybe?

The power to influence your future is in your hands *right now*. You could achieve a more successful, happier future simply by changing something that you are doing right now.

Take action now!

QUICK PLAN

- **What is your ideal goal/vision? Write it down and place it around your house to serve as a reminder.**

- **Practice your meditation every morning to put yourself in a good strong state every morning.**

UNDERSTAND

THE REBEL WITHIN

STEP NINE

Understand the Rebel Within

Your attitude and behavior will determine how much
and what kind of respect a person will have for you.
Rashida Rowe

Bad habits may appear in so many forms. One is that of being the rebel.

Many psychologists believe that everyone possesses a little rebel in their personality. This characteristic comes to life when you disregard the rules or don't want to accept authority. Yes, it is the 'going against the grain' part that associates people with being a rebel.

Sometimes, a rebellious nature results from deep-seated frustration. It is possible to become a rebel towards yourself. Think back to when you are striving to achieve something and you keep coming across blockages or challenges that make that journey towards the goal seem almost unachievable. Can you recall how frustrated you felt? Have you ever heard anyone complaining that it is almost too difficult to achieve something and then you find them starting to question the worth of the goal in the first place? How about when you go on a diet?

Jane worked in an office full of other women. There was a great atmosphere in the office and all of them got on very well with each other. It was the kind of office that always seemed to have some delicious cake in it that one of the team had baked for her colleagues and friends. Consequently, there were times when one or more would suddenly announce that they needed to go on a diet and try to abstain from the cake. Jane was no different. She felt that was putting on a few extra pounds so announced to everyone that she was going to be resolute in her weight loss goal. She started bringing in healthy salads to eat. It was fine for the first few days, perhaps even the first week or two. She had her salad while others ate the office cake. It didn't bother her in the slightest but secretly she did wish that they would bring in healthy food instead so that they could all lose weight together. Unfortunately, the others were feeling fine with the cake and continued to bring it in. It was only a matter of time before Jane started to get really bored of her salads. Her weight wasn't coming down quick enough and she wasn't having as much fun at work. All of her friends were cooing over the latest cake and took great pleasure in eating it over their morning coffee break.

Soon, Jane started to question the point of the weight loss. She wasn't obese after all. She was healthy and her husband didn't complain about her size. Why was she putting herself through this nonsense diet? She asked her colleagues and they also said that they didn't see that she was overweight or needed to diet. That's when the rebel voice inside her head started getting louder and louder, questioning the point of dieting when there is nothing wrong with her or why should she bother trying to diet when there was always cake available at work? Eventually, Jane gave up on the diet and joined her friends in the office cake once more. The diet became simply a distant memory. Jane had self-sabotaged as a result of the rebel within.

The term rebel is often associated with teenagers through that much-dreaded puberty phase. If you've had a teenager in your life you will know what I mean. The moment that a teenager tests your patience by being seemingly irrational and by blatantly ignoring rules, then you would be forgiven for thinking that a rebel has started to blossom.

The social pressure, the search for personal identity, the overall environment – all of these contribute to the development of this habit. It's important to note here that being a rebel is not always a guaranteed bad habit. The following are cultural/social norms of having the rebel-like habit:

THE POSITIVES

1. **A rebel always finds courage in overwhelming circumstance.** A rebel is somehow ready to take on any challenge no matter how difficult a situation seems to be.

2. **A rebel has a built-in energy production system.** Despite going against the flow, a rebel always has an unceasing supply of energy that allow him/her to relentlessly pursue what they believe to be right.

3. **A rebel is an original thinker.** You can't expect a rebel to opt for the *status quo*. It goes against the very concept. He is the bearer of unique ideas that could be a bit too much to accept for others. However, when it comes to originality, a rebel could really surprise you.

4. **A rebel's viewpoint allows you to re-think yours**. Having a rebel within your group can

be an advantage. You may use their ideas to validate your own.

THE NEGATIVES

1. **Rebels do not recognise a punishment as 'punishment'**. Rebels, by their nature, are likely to regard punishment as weak or unjust. Most often, they also tend to break the same 'rules' over and over again. For example, a rebellious teenager who gets grounded for breaking a curfew law is more likely to repeat it than a conformist.

2. **Rebels tend to be more solitary**. Rebels prefer to work independently, not because they hate the idea of being a part of a group but, because they feel more productive when they do so. They are especially frustrated with people who are conformists. I recognise this myself. As a rebel, I identified myself as being 'different' to others and I used to get quite frustrated with conformists and bureaucracy. This facet of being a rebel is not completely negative.

The development of the rebellious mindset does not happen overnight. There could be a triggering factor, social, biological or environmental, that hits the rebellion button. Kids only see what their parents do and they quickly associate them with their parents' concept of right and wrong. However, as they grow, they become more and more exposed to other external influences, such as their peers, popular culture and teachers, that causes them to redefine their beliefs.

So how do you deal with rebellious teenagers? You may want to consider these ideas:

1. Spend time together. Instead of letting your children go to school by bus, offer to drive them to school once in a while. A few minutes together in the morning can offer a great opportunity to talk.
2. Understand your child's interests and friends. Genuinely get to know what interests them most.
3. Recognise your kid's effort at school. We all want to be recognised and rewarded for our hard work. I'm not talking about buying expensive gifts but never underestimate the power of your words and compliments.
4. Communicate without nagging. No one likes to be nagged and everyone appreciates it when others make a genuine effort to

understand their position.

5. Dealing with a rebel at work can be tricky. Show the person that you respect their opinion even if you do not agree with them completely. This can diffuse any tension.

6. Give your rebel subordinate sufficient space to work by himself, but do not cordon him off completely from the team. Remember, if you always do what you've always done you will always get what you've always got. Rebels can be the source of new ideas.

7. Never start a debate with a rebel. You probably won't win, no matter how logical or right you are. Asserting that you are right and that the rebel is wrong would most likely leave a feeling of frustration or anger towards you or the company.

How do people respond to you (when you are the rebel)? More importantly, how do you treat yourself when you are being the rebel?

Being a rebel can be detrimental to the kind of future you want for yourself and for your family. Granted, there are some positives. However, it is essential to understand the repercussion it has in your own life and in the life you share with other people. Be open to the idea of addressing your rebellious behaviour. And be firm on the idea of being socially and mentally healthy for your own good.

QUICK PLAN

- **Keep a daily journal of thoughts as you progress through your journey to identify the inner language that you think comes from the inner rebel.**

- **Tip – try to reframe these thoughts to reflect the opposite of what they might be (it makes for a great game to pass the time and helps to reshape your language.)**

HONOUR
YOURSELF

STEP TEN

Honour Yourself

"If only you could sense how important you are to the lives of those you meet; how important you can be to people you may never even dream of. There is something of yourself that you leave at every meeting with another person."

Fred Rogers

Do you go round beating yourself up all the time? How much do you value yourself?

If you don't see yourself as strong or capable, how will you change your behaviour and break your bad habits? It is always a positive act to honour yourself. It comes with the belief that you can make a change and that you have the power within you to move forward.

Okay, so let's get on the same page here. First and foremost we need to *accept* who we are. We need to learn our strengths and weaknesses and then **accept** them. In short, we need to learn to love and appreciate ourselves. Be your own best friend. After all, you spend more time with yourself than anybody else in your whole life.

Make a list of all of your strengths; all the stuff that you are awesome at, no matter how small or freaky and tell yourself that you are the best in the world at being you. No one else could get anywhere close.

Don't sweat the small stuff. No one in this world is perfect. All the greatest achievers in this world have made mistakes and learned from them to move forward. So can you!

This section will look at the emotion of guilt and how you can fight against it instead of putting yourself down.

Why Guilt or Frustration Does Not Work.

Guilt in any which way cannot be a valid reason to change bad habits. All it achieves is to stop you from taking the right steps to achieve the changes you wanted. Being guilty leads to nowhere. It's a waste of your energy.

Your mind is more powerful than anything else in the world. What you think about you bring about. As guilt is a negative emotion, you are allowing the powerhouse that is your mind to bring about more stuff into your life to regret in the future. Since you might not be aware that guilt is already affecting you, here are some points to help you recognise the symptoms:

- Regularly thinking about the past with feelings of regret or pain.
- Justifying your behaviour all the time.
- Being defensive about your life when questioned.
- Hating or disliking yourself every time you look in the mirror

Where Does the Guilty Feeling Come From?

Not all values instilled within your mind are all yours. Everything we know today has been learned from other people. It's called 'conditioning'. From the moment we are born we are surrounded by people influencing us, from our parents, our teachers, siblings through to the adverts that we see on television and the books we read

Most of the time, this knowledge and the standards that we aspire to are good. However, very often we end up measuring ourselves against these standards and find that we are lacking. This leads us to experience negative feelings about ourselves or our position in life.

That is when our guilt and feeling of

inadequacy kicks in to make us feel really bad about ourselves.

We can blame others for 'making' us feel guilty but, in truth, only we are responsible for our own thoughts. No one can *make* you feel anything. We choose our emotions, whether we like it or not. Only *we* will make ourselves feel guilty, although others might influence that in us.

However, knowing this, we can also take charge of our thoughts. We can *choose* to feel good about ourselves. We can become the best versions of ourselves, if we choose to be. That is the level of power that we have within us. If you stop and think about it, you realise how truly awesome this is. Just by changing our mindset we could transform our lives. Every time I think about it, it sends shivers up my spine.

Where do you go with guilt?

Guilt can very often lead you to become angry with yourself which can lead to more negative places rather than positive. Anger is such a negative emotion and is more than likely going to prevent you from moving forward, rather than drive the change you want to see.

My simple advice is to stop ruining your life with senseless guilt!

Focus on Strength and Confidence

A person who lacks self-confidence is less likely to achieve than one who has a power of self-belief. You may have heard the old Henry Ford quote, *"Whether you think you can, or you think you can't you are right."* Our actions and our results are in direct proportion to our level of self-belief.

You have your own strength but only you can develop it.

You've probably heard about affirmations. You know, phrases that you repeatedly use to move and inspire yourself to move forwards. The more you affirm to yourself that you can do something, the more likely you are to achieve it. However, affirmations can also be negative when reinforced as limiting beliefs. Bob says, 'There is no way on earth I can achieve that." Really? Why is Bob so convinced he can't achieve something he has never even tried?

It's all based on your inner language and conversation. The experiences and conditioning that you've experienced throughout your life develop a set of beliefs in you that then guide you throughout the rest of your life. If your parents always told you that rich people are ruthless and step on other people to acquire their fortunes, how likely are you to ever trust a wealthy person?

If you were told that real friends are hard to come by and it became your belief, how likely are you to make a good circle of friends that you whole heartedly trust?

Forget about the line that says – "No, I can't do it" or "I am weak in this area or that area" or "I would love to do that but I just couldn't because…[add your own limiting belief in here]".

Ask yourself what the real evidence is behind these limiting beliefs. Be honest with yourself. Challenge that little voice inside your head because, more often than not, we have no direct evidence that the belief is actually true.

Kick that thinking into touch! You are far more capable of change than you ever thought you were.

If you want to find out more about affirmations, download the free book on my website at **www.kulmahay.com**.

Re-building Your Strength and Confidence

If you think you can't change your bad habits and honour yourself because you are weak or you are afraid, do not forget that you have your strengths that are just hiding beneath the surface within you. This untapped resource is just waiting for you to use it. Unleash it and watch the remarkable power that you have. It's a bit like an oil field gusher – once it starts, it never seems to want to stop and our life will become much, much richer.

Re-build and use your strength to be able to honour yourself and follow these pointers.

- Practice honesty with yourself at all times.
- Admit your fear and then demonstrate courage by moving forward
- What others think is their story, what you think is your choice
- See and feel the guilt leaving you

What can you ask yourself?

Self-analysis is critical if you are to change the way you behave and to move towards massive change by eliminating habits that have held you back for so long. These questions might help you to examine yourself:

1. *Why did I have the habit in the first place?* This question will help you understand yourself better. If you are truly honest with yourself, you are likely to realise that your

reason for the habit now sounds pretty feeble at best.

2. *What were you like when you practised the habit*? This might help to understand the impact you were having on yourself and others.

3. *Why did I really start this habit?* Was it because **I** wanted it or because **others** influenced me? Remember, it is always you who is responsible for how you live your life.

Do it with all your strength

Self-belief, therefore, is critical to achieving anything in life, including breaking negative cycles of behaviour that affect your life. From self-belief arises strength which will most definitely take you to a whole new life.

Some simple pointers to practice regularly would be to:

- Be conscious – Actively be aware of your thoughts and your actions
- Be authentic – Be honest with yourself at the deepest level
- Be responsible – You have choices. No one can make you do anything. You choose so take responsibility for your

choices

You are assured in winning the battle to fight the feeling of guilt in changing your bad habits if you use your strength effectively!

Remember, sometimes the bad habit is just the pattern of our self-talk. You can change that habit just like all the other physical habits we have looked at.

QUICK PLAN

- Ask yourself the 3 questions to explore why you started the habit and its impact on your life.

- Make a list of all of your positive traits and achievements throughout your life. This might be an ongoing thing you do as part of daily journal.

HAVE A CLEAR
STRATEGY

STEP ELEVEN

Have a Clear Strategy

A man who does not plan long ahead will find trouble at his door."

Confucius

Okay, but you've already gone through the previous 10 steps. By now you should have identified your habit, understood how it affects your life, put a project plan in place towards achieving your desired result. If you've got to this point in the book, I'm guessing you have done a lot of soul searching and realized that you really do want this habit out of your life. You are ready to begin your transformation.

There are so many ways of fighting habits that I have seen used but, take it from me, none of them are ever going to work over night. Until, some miracle cure comes to light, we have to accept that it takes time, patience and hard work to make this happen. There has to be a clear commitment from the person themselves to break the habit. The level of commitment is directly proportional to the amount of desire and passion one has. Even so, please, please do not expect overnight success. It is a journey on which we have embarked together.

You might find this disheartening or disappointing but, if you really are serious about getting your life back, it is important to understand that any kind of transformation is a journey full of smaller goals, or milestones.

To rid yourself of negative behaviour that has been holding you back for some time, it is important to create a plan. Getting rid of the bad habit is not just about stopping it and then congratulating yourself on your success (although it would be important to celebrate this as a key milestone).

It's more than that. How many times have you heard of someone who has tried the latest extreme diet to lose weight in 7 days? Most of the time, they make amazing changes to their size, shape and weight, don't they? Yet, do they maintain that lesser weight? My experience is that the vast majority who change their habits in extremely short timescales with extreme practices, end up going back to those very same habits within a couple of months. 'Why is that?' you might ask. Good question.

If you are changing your whole way of living in a very short time, it is going to be very difficult to maintain it. It hasn't been incorporated in a way of life. It is relatively easy to be focused over a short span of time to achieve noticeable results but you haven't necessarily introduced your body and mind to a longer term sustainable way of life. In fact, what tends to happen is that your cravings for that habit have simply been held in abeyance and when you stop that 7 day detox, diet or whatever else it is. The accumulated cravings suddenly burst the dam of self-restraint and rush in. You tend to over indulge, perhaps even more than before, on the habit that you crave. This is why, very often, we find that those who go for 7 day dramatic diet plans are likely to increase their weight quite rapidly after they have completed it. Perhaps even more than they were before the diet.

The best results tend to be from those who have incorporated it into their daily lifestyle. They have created something that is sustainable.

What is the right approach to stop your bad habit?

Acceptance – Before you can change your bad habit you must accept that something is wrong and that you need to change your behaviour. In general, those people who were able to recover successfully are those who really accept the truth about themselves.

Ask for support – Doing something by yourself can sometimes feel like an uphill battle. It's not enough that you want to stop and rehabilitate yourself. Find people who can support, encourage and coach you through the process. There are support groups for most things now and are readily able to share your journey. Failing that, we have already discussed having supportive mentors to hold your hand through the journey to becoming habit-free.

Have a Time Frame to Follow

Remember the **SMART** action plan technique we discussed earlier in the book? This would be a great opportunity to think about it now.

To assist your thinking in developing a strategy just consider a few simple questions that might help to focus you:

1. What is your ultimate vision? What do you

want to achieve? Imagine what your life would look like without the bad habit in your life. Which aspects of your life would it affect? Would it impact on your relationships, your health, or perhaps your finances? Look at your potential life in as much detail as you can. How do the changes resulting from you losing your habit affect your life? How would you feel in this 'new life'?

2. Why do you want to achieve this amazing new life? Once you have understood that the life which you are heading for is one that is habit-free and full of new opportunities, be clear as to why you want that life? By doing this, you will help to create passion within yourself which, in turn, helps you to constantly focus on your goal and take the action required of you.

3. What are your milestones? Like any great project, you will need points in time that you can focus on in the near future. It will help with the focus and energise you to go further. I do this both for myself and for my coaching clients. Simply in writing this book, for example, each chapter is a milestone for me. It means I'm getting closer to my ultimate destination. Once I have completed my writing, there are several other milestones built in,

such as getting my illustrations completed, the cover designed, the various stages of editing, formatting and then published. You get the picture? Every journey has milestones. Imagine you are travelling to another country. Don't you have milestones built in? You get to the airport, you check-in and secure your seat, you get through security, you spend some time in the departure lounge, you get to the boarding gate and then you board your plane. Each of these steps mean that you are getting closer to your holiday destination. How do you feel each time you complete one more step? Relieved, excited? That's exactly how it should be for this 'journey' that you are undertaking. Set a series of milestones all the way to your final destination and remember to celebrate each milestone because it means you are that bit closer to your goal!

The importance of having a plan

Once you have made a blueprint of your self-reconstruction, test your plan. Share it with others. Be honest with yourself about its achievability.

You may have people to support you but this fight is yours. It's important that you have a plan that you can work to and commit to that has a clear path to your success. This plan is your footpath to success so be ruthless in your commitment to it.

Know that if you were just able to keep to your plan, you would most definitely be habit-free and have an amazing new life.

No one will ever feel the hurt of withdrawing from the substance of your bad habit more than you. That's why your blueprint must be very effective and reliable to help you. Also your plan must fit well to your goal to change.

All the rules being implanted into your blueprint will provide you with a complete assessment of yourself. Once you have a plan, your tendency to lead yourself astray is less likely. Planning your self-improvement is a good investment, after completing the course you will appreciate life more.

QUICK PLAN

- **Develop your ultimate vision – describe exactly what you want your life to look like once you are habit-free**

- **Ask yourself why you want this**

- **Review the milestones in your SMART plan to ensure they are on track and taking you towards your goal**

TAKE MASSIVE ACTION

STEP TWELVE

Take Massive Action

"Vision without action is merely a dream.
Action without vision just passes the time.
Vision with action can change the world."

Joel A. Barker

Focus. Now that you are aware of your bad habits, have recognised them and have decided to go all the way to change them, you should start thinking about it. After you have your plan in place, you must stick to it ruthlessly and get to your goal. Remember to focus on this plan and try your absolute best.

What to focus on?

What do you have to focus on? Simply the things you have planned to do. Focus on the things you want to achieve, on your goals, on the future you want to have and the benefits of stopping this bad habit. Focus on your next milestone. Think of the things you could to do to achieve this goal. You can start by focusing on an image of your future self after you have achieved your successful outcome. Think of the effects of the things you are doing now to your future; that ought to help you a lot. Find something you want to achieve and set that as your goal to focus on.

How to focus?

Starting to focus is really hard at first but, after you have clarified with yourself the small goals along the way, it will become much easier. Trust me. Just think of that next thing you want to focus on. Do this at every part of your journey; every time you are executing your plan.

Just consider all the things you want or have. Remember that the past is something that should not be forgotten but something we should not be stuck in either. You just have to carry the lessons you have learned in the past into your bright, new future, full of amazing potential. The future is something you *can* look forward to. Try to focus on these things that you see in your future and just keep moving forward. Be relentless in your journey towards the new, improved future self.

How to maintain focus?

Now that you have started focusing yourself on the things you want, you must maintain that focus. So how do you do this? The answer lies within yourself. You keep doing exactly what you were doing yesterday when you were focusing or a while ago when you did something according to plan. **Make your plan the new habit**. Become the addict of self-improvement.

Start Changing

From the very start, when you have just acknowledged the need to change your behaviour, you have started the process of change.

'There is an old saying that every journey of a thousand miles starts with a single step'. More often than not, that step is the decision to take the journey in the first place.

If you are reading this book, it means that you have made a decision to take some sort of change in your life. You have already started the journey. Congratulations! You have started the change process, perhaps without even realising it.

Make up your mind

I know that you have your plan ready now. Great stuff!

How confident are you in your plan? I can't stress enough that the plan has to be realistic, achievable, measurable and achievable (refer back to the **SMART** plan description.)

A **SMART** plan will allow you to see real results as you move forward and keep you motivated through your successes of yesterday.

With the achievement of each milestone go crazy with excitement!! Jump up and down, punch the air. Do whatever you need to do to show to yourself that you are moving forward in your life.

I'm feeling tremors of excitement just writing this section knowing that you are going to be moving forward. Just do it!!

Take Action - Execute that plan!

Now you have your plan and you are focused, determined and really excited. Go ahead and EXECUTE your plan. Go kick start your plan! If you want to stop smoking, go throw those cigarettes away. Some people make this a ritual. I remember a client who decided that she wanted to have a midnight symbolic burning of her cigarettes in a small bonfire in her garden. It doesn't matter how you do it, how crazy it might seem to others, just do it. Remember that moment that you got rid of the bottles of booze in your home, the moment you cleared your refrigerator of the junk and the sugary foods that were taking up so much space.

Remember that this is a new day. Go buy some healthy fruit juices, put some cool water in your fridge with pieces of refreshing and detoxifying lemon or lime in it.

I remember doing this about 6 months ago when I purged myself of my sugary drinks and coffee. Now I drink nothing but lemon water. I'm on 5 pints a day and I feel awesome!!

You can do it! You will be able to do it as long as you trust yourself and think that you can.

If your habit is that you tend to get frustrated easily with people and resort to shouting at others, commit to continue shouting but only in praise. Make other people's day and give yourself the pleasure of knowing that you are changing bit by bit. Not only that, notice how you feel when you see the reaction in others that you are now praising and encouraging them. Watch how they flourish and grow themselves. All because of you! How cool is that?!

You may not see the outcome as fast as you might want but when you look at it in the bigger picture, the small ripples you make will soon create this giant splash that will bring a change into the company or community around you.

Start small, always. Don't rush things and things will all fall into their right places. This is a marathon, not a sprint.

Try your best

Whatever plan you have, it will work out. Just try your best in whatever you do. Give it your all and know that things will go just fine.

I'm reminded of a great quote here by the successful restauranteur, Stephen Kaggwa,

"Successful people aren't born that way. They become successful by establishing the habit of doing things unsuccessful people don't like to do. The successful people don't always like these things themselves; they just get on and do them."

Remember to smile and enjoy

What you are doing, you are doing for yourself, so don't attach any negative emotions to it, like guilt, anger or frustration or anything like that. Things are meant to go wrong along the way, so just accept whatever might happen. Smile! Enjoy doing the things you have planned to do. The only competitor you have is yourself. Don't compare yourself with others; we are all on different journeys, no matter how similar they might appear.

Smile, knowing that at the end of the day, you will be able to look people straight in the eye and say "I've changed for the better". Smile, knowing that the process may not be easy but it will certainly pay off! More importantly, smile because you know that you have become a better version of yourself.

QUICK PLAN

- **Take action every single day!**

- **Review your action against your plan throughout the day**

- **Read your vision notes to remind you why you are doing this.**

- **Continue to practice your meditation daily**

SWITCH BAD HABITS FOR GOOD

STEP THIRTEEN

Switching Habits For Good

"Change might not be fast and it isn't always easy. But with time and effort, almost any habit can be reshaped."

Charles Duhigg

Identify Your Bad Habit

The hardest part of breaking away from bad habits is identifying them. Hard as it is, it is still the most significant step. Some people call it soul searching but it doesn't need to be so spiritually orientated that you feel you need to go to a retreat or disappear into the mountains (but if it's good for you to really look within yourself then, hey, why not?) For most people, this can simply be finding some time to sit down in a quiet place and to really internalise their thoughts. It might help to write down those thoughts and the commitments to the changes that you make.

The first step in identifying your bad habits is

admitting that you *have* bad habits. Simply because if you can't admit it, you are telling yourself that you don't have a bad habit. Therefore, there is nothing to change in the first place. However, I think we can safely assume that, if you are reading this book, you have already identified a habit you want to break free from.

No more excuses! Let's be honest with ourselves. You know yourself! Ask yourself what bad habits you need to break away from. You can also ask your friends and loved ones for some honest feedback (it might be very uncomfortable to hear it, but at least you know where your starting point is). Consolidate your thoughts and ponder on their opinions. From there, you can assess what habits you need to say goodbye to.

We also need to ask if our habits causes harm to others. Are our practical jokes funny or annoying? I'm reminded of the lyrics to a beautiful Bee Gees song, 'I started a Joke'

I started a joke
which started the whole world crying
But I didn't see that the joke was on me oh no
I started to cry
which started the whole world laughing
Oh If I'd only seen that the joke was on me

What if our habit of making fun really hurts others? Can we truly say it is just a joke or fun?

In today's world, this kind of bad habit is now called "bullying" and it now receives so much attention that in some places there is a law against bullying.

No excuses! Let's be honest with ourselves and be true. You know yourself! The only person that truly knows you and your habits is yourself. Once you've identified your bad habits, it's the right time to replace your bad habits with good habits.

Replacing your Bad Habit with a Good One

Now that have we identified our bad habits it's time to replace it with a good one. Believe me, it is never too late to switch bad habits for good ones.

Every habit will have an opposite. Think about your habit. What would it's opposite be?

Do you have a bad habit of having incessant sexual desires? What about a bad habit of going to bed without cleaning your body, like brushing teeth, washing your hands or face? What if you just leave a mess in your house every time you go to bed, like dirty plates in the sink (by the way, did you know that this was a great way of attracting ants and spiders into your home?) With these kind of habits, we could reframe them and practice,

129

cleanliness or purity.

Let's purify our desires, practice cleanliness of both material things and of ourselves. In our minds and in our body.

How great does it feel knowing that your house is clean (I'm not talking about that clinical feeling but a general feeling of tidiness) when you wake up in the morning? I used to be terrible. I would leave pots and pans in the kitchen sink and cushions scattered everywhere in my lounge. It literally takes me 5-10 minutes to clear things away before bedtime now and I still love the feeling of waking up to a lovely clean house.

I don't know about you but when I shower before bed, I feel more refreshed and sleep even deeper, waking up feeling more energised and relaxed.

Do you have a big appetite? I used to! I was constantly eating and drinking throughout the day. Not wine or beer (I decided to stop drinking some twelve years ago and have never looked back because I feel so great now) but I did end up drinking a lot of sugary drinks or coffee. I switched this to drinking lemon water and green tea about 6 months ago. I can honestly say that I have never felt so good. The energy from the alkalising effect on my body and the detoxifying from the lemon really has helped me to feel great in myself.

The other side of having a big appetite is to buy luxuriously. We are surrounded and bombarded by hypnotic commercials (trust me, I'm a hypnotist) that tell us we need to buy the latest clothes, cars, gadgets and toys. The truth is that we might not even need them but we buy them because they give us a sudden rush of pleasure that we have acquired something new to own.

It is a fleeting, temporary pleasure but one we can easily get addicted to because we are soon looking for the next thing to buy that will make us feel great.

How about trying this? Rather than acquiring things all the time, experience the real joy of giving. It doesn't matter what you give, a possession, money, or simply your time. Try to give regularly to those who are less fortunate than you are. There are plenty of charities out there crying out for help, plenty of homeless people who would benefit from a hot meal or lonely people around you who would love for someone to just sit and talk to them for a few minutes. A few weeks ago, I heard of the plight of refugees in Europe. I decided I wanted to take action and put a post on Facebook. I was shocked by the sheer response. I filled a van with donations which I will be taking to France later this week. In the process, I have made a whole new group of friends.

Once you have given, you will understand the level of joy you experience that is a much longer lasting feeling than simply acquiring the next item of clothing.

Do you have a habit of "I'll do it later"? Procrastination, laziness, or whatever you choose to call it, is one heck of a bad habit. How do we undo this behaviour?

Well firstly, we need to understand and agree that the opposite of procrastinating or being lazy is to be productive. Productivity leads to increased performance which can only lead to better results. Agree?

Suddenly it becomes a no-brainer. Let's be persistent in our work and be passionate about it. Let us make more effort to do what is right. Finally, imagine the rewards we can get by becoming much more productive in our lives.

The struggle with habits is not new. It goes back over thousands of years. All religions will have their individual set of capital sins that worshippers are encouraged to avoid, such as lust, anger, greed, ego and attachment. For thousands of years we have tried to overcome negative behaviour and, whilst the language might have changed, the same things that we battle with in today's modern society were present then. The really crazy thing is how simple the switching of behaviours and habits might be and the potential for increased rewards at the end of it all.

It is really all about re-framing your language. Think about the habit you want to get rid of. Consider what its opposite would be. Commit to becoming the addict of the opposite. It is as simple as that (although, as we already know it will require action and effort on your part).

Importance of Replacing the Habit

Why is it important to replace our bad habits? Not just to be good but to feel good too. Bad habits can be such a heavy burden. Both on yourself and others.

I once met a little 8 year old boy who still sucked his thumb as if it were a baby pacifier. His parents were fed up of telling him to stop. This simple habit was affecting everyone concerned. The parents were embarrassed when others questioned their ability in bringing up their child and the poor boy was being picked on and bullied by other kids at school.

Replacing your bad habits creates a new image of you. People see a different you every time they see you. If that happens, new opportunities come too. Good habits open new doors for you, for your work or profession, even in school if you are a student. Let me use smoking as a simple example.

Some people don't like smokers (I know this as I smoked myself for 21 years before finally making the shift). They don't like to inhale the smoke, they don't the smell of the cigarettes as it clings to their clothes and you can't blame them, can you?

How often do you find others avoid having conversations with you up close while you are smoking? How many people are there in your life, in whose company you don't smoke? Why is that? If we are true to ourselves, it is because we know they don't like it but we value their company sufficiently not to smoke around them. I know. I did exactly that as a smoker, myself.

Other smokers simply detach themselves from those who do not like smoking. As a result they don't develop what could have been great relationships. That's pretty sad, don't you think?

What I'm trying to say is that your habits, whether good or bad, define you as a person and your personality. That is why when you recognise your bad habits or someone tells you have a bad habit, have a serious think about it. Apply all the techniques we have already looked at and think about how to replace it as part of your overall strategy to smash it.

QUICK PLAN

- **Consider the opposite to your bad habit and use it as an additional goal to strive for.**

ENLIST SUPPORT

STEP FOURTEEN

Enlist Support

*The cares of this life can consume you if you
depend on self. You need the comforter who will
uplift the standard
against all odds and give you peace.*
Wilson Khashane Msendevu

As a Life Change Specialist, I know the value that my clients get from my coaching and support to change their current lifestyles to move forward to a whole new amazing, transformed life.

Having that support from someone else is really invaluable and, whilst we have touched upon it earlier in the book, it really deserves a chapter in its own right, such is the value of it.

It's best that we enlist a people support system or our own network of either professional or personal contacts that will help to guide and motivate us in achieving our goal of breaking our bad habits.

'Why?' you may ask. It's because doing it alone makes no one accountable for our actions but ourselves and, yes, this is the main reason why we tend to go back to our old ways and old habits. We can all too easily allow ourselves to make up excuses for not having achieved goals or milestones.

We might think that, since no one else knows of our supposed resolve to defeat this bad habit, it makes it easier to procrastinate or fall back.

On the other hand, making your goal known to others will also make you accountable for its accomplishment. Remember, we do not have to do this alone.

So, who are those people that we can enlist to help battle our bad habits?

1. Support from family members/friends

Who can influence and provide us with the support that we need in handling our bad habits? They are those people that are closest to us and who know us personally and want the very best for us.

Our family. Our family have known us longer than anyone else as they have been with us since day one. They have been there with us even before that habit became a bad habit. If we are really committed to enforce the lifestyle changes then it's best to keep them close at hand as allies.

Our friends. Friends serve as our second family and they are our major influencers in who we currently are. If, for instance, our bad habit is something that we can't tell our family out of the fear that they will think less of us, or whatever the reason might be, we can always turn to our friends for support. However, be careful in choosing who, out of your friends, you should seek help from. It's best to consider those that you're closest to. Choose friends who you are comfortable with, have been with you through thick and thin and who you know will have your best interests at heart and would be prepared to be tough with you, should you flag a bit.

Our family and friends can help us deal with our bad habits in a number of ways:

- *We can ask them to hold us to account.* Say they caught us cracking our fingers or smoking, we can give them permission to reprimand or remind us of what exactly our goals are.
- *We can talk to them.* Since we trust them, we can tell them everything. We can always talk

to them personally or call them whenever we feel that we are being drawn to our bad habit. Be honest with them and make sure they will be honest with you too. Remember that old saying, "A problem shared is a problem halved"?

- *They can be our quality control.* Let family and friends know how this change is of importance to you. If, for instance, you have the bad habit of eating sweets whenever you are bored, they can help by eliminating sweets from the shopping list. They can help limit your time watching television if you are prone to procrastinate and watch too much of it.

Sharing our bad habit challenges with family and friends drives us closer to them as our relationship bond strengthens.

2. Professional Help

Another way of getting a support system in place is by seeking professional help and this includes counsellors, doctors, coaches or a support group. More often than not, this additional resource puts everything on to a much more focused, professional footing. A clear commitment towards banishing this habit forever.

Who are the professionals that we can turn to and how can they help?

Coaches.

Getting a coach is a very effective strategy. Being accountable to others forces a person to push harder and to stay focused on the goal. The fact that you actually paid to avail of their services adds to the motivation. The coach will help you to look at your situation much deeper than you have in the past, work with you to arrive at some milestones and to understand your ultimate goal. Be prepared though. A good coach will hold you to account for the actions that you have committed to performing. I know. I have had to have some strong conversations with errant clients in the past but, trust me, coaches only have the client's best interests at heart.

Counsellors

Counsellors will explore with you your fears, mental obstacles and doubts and help to arrive at some coping strategies to move forward.

This, in a way, will help you stay on the track. Working with your counsellor will help you figure out other factors (like stressors for instance) that might have significance to your bad habits and also find healthy and positive ways of dealing with them.

Medical Professionals.

Breaking a bad habit by yourself can be very difficult especially if it's related to substance dependency, such as drugs, smoking or alcohol. Other habits for which medical advice would be very important are things like eating disorders or self-harming. I guess the simple rule is that if your habit is affecting your health, go see a doctor.

Support group.

Sometimes, hearing and getting advice from people who have undergone the same issues is more preferable as you can relate to their past experiences, and knowing that they have actually conquered the battle can be very inspiring.

People link up with others who are trying to make the same changes and eventually they lend each other encouragement and support.

Support groups have regular meetings and they gather at different locations at all times of the day. They are informed about other people who have been successful and they try to learn from these people's experiences.

Check to see if there is a support group holding meetings near you. You might also try looking on

Facebook – you will be amazed at the variety of groups available on social media. I'm sure you can find one closer to you than you imagined.

3. Spiritual Advice

If you are close to your religion, you might consider spiritual counselling from your local religious leader or teacher.

I know many people who have found solace in this, particularly with habits that have a moral or social context to them, e.g. swearing, gossiping, lying, etc.

Here, the emphasis is likely to be on the responsibility we have for our own thoughts and actions and that we asking God for guidance. Spiritual advice focuses mainly with our relationship with God.

Many find this level of support and guidance of great comfort at a time when they are feeling challenged and I strongly recommend exploring it as an option.

Overall, changing our bad habits is really difficult as it takes time and effort. We might not be likely to get rid of it all the first time (as no one is perfect) but with perseverance and the helping relationships around us, chances are it should be more bearable and more likely to succeed. Nothing is impossible as long as you are serious about overcoming your bad habits once and for all.

QUICK PLAN

- **Identify which family member/friend that you will share your plan with and ask them to support you**

- **Research support groups in your area that might assist you**

- **Consider the use of a professional coach/ counsellor/medical expert to support you**

- **Search for and join relevant groups on social media**

REWARD YOURSELF

STEP FIFTEEN

Reward Yourself

To be a champion you have to believe in yourself
When no one else will
Sugar Ray Robinson

What is a Reward System?
This is a very useful way of staying on track by giving yourself a reward as you progress towards breaking a bad habit or succeeding in something. Rewarding yourself is very important, especially after you have successfully taken yourself onto that positive path you have chosen. It's not easy to commit yourself to breaking a habit that you are so used to and it will take a lot of courage and hard work to start the journey. That's why a reward for you would be a great treat.

Sometimes, this reward may come from you or sometimes it comes from other people who saw you strive and try your best to achieve the goal. With this reward system, you have something to look forward to at the end of each milestone.

You can use the reward system as a form of encouragement for yourself to overcome the challenges in order for you to be successful. These rewards will help you push yourself more and work harder in trying to break that bad habit. After a day of trying to keep yourself from the temptation of smoking, treating yourself to your favourite food could be a great reward. With this reward that you have set up for yourself, you may come to realise that your hard work does pay off. At the very least, you get the encouragement to continue this the next day because you know you'll get another reward for fighting your negative urges.

How or what you reward yourself is actually up to you. You can instantly give yourself the reward after the first day that you have demonstrated that extreme self-control.

The important thing is that you are taking steady steps forward. You might want to add a reward to each milestone celebration. The reward is there to show you how far you have come and, by the very fact that you are rewarding yourself, you are travelling in the right direction.

How about putting the money you might spend

on a habit, such as smoking, eating, shopping, drinking, into a glass jar and at every milestone you treat yourself to something indulgent (but good) like a massage treatment or a manicure? For the fellas, it could be a day out somewhere like a day in a sports car or karting. You will be amazed at how much money you are spending on your habit, directly or indirectly, so make sure you account for every penny and squirrel it away or give it to one of your trusted supporters to do it for you and then treat yourself and/or your loved ones to something nice. We all like to be spoilt every now and then, don't we?

Importance of Rewarding

Now that you have taken the first step in trying to break your bad trait, no matter if it's a small or huge success, you should celebrate it. You deserve that!! It is essential to celebrate big or small milestones in your life especially now that you are well on the road to finally breaking that bad habit. Why are these rewards so important? They are important because they will actually help you focus more on your goal and motivate you to move in the right direction. Why? Because they give you something in the future to work towards and look forward to. This in itself is a great motivator. With each reward, you will have the inspiration and courage to do the same tomorrow.

Focus on what or how you will treat yourself at the next milestone to shift your thoughts from the habit towards thinking about success.

Think of treating yourself to something for not smoking a single cigarette the whole day. Make sure it's something that is good and not reinforcing the habit, itself. For instance, don't reward yourself with a cigarette to celebrate one week of being smoke-free. That sounds ridiculous, right? Trust me, I've met plenty who have done just that (including me before I finally decided to stop smoking).

Make it something that you will look forward to and keep it in your mind to keep you motivated throughout the day. It might also help you *not* to think about the habit by keeping your mind focused.

Sometimes, a cheer or congratulatory message for you is enough of a reward. Never under estimate the power of genuine praise from those who love or care for you. If someone from your circle of friends or a member of the family knows that you are trying to break a bad habit and they see how much work you are putting into breaking free, even a "good job" or "well done" from them or a simple tap at your back can make a huge difference. It will motivate you even more to stay on track.

How to Decide What Reward is best

When choosing a reward, it should be something that is not related to the habit you are trying to get rid of. The reward can be something small or something grand, however you like it. As long as it gives you the motivation to keep going on the next day, it is a good reward.

There is no real right or wrong here. It should be something that you really like or want. These small tokens or rewards for yourself will actually work if you give them to yourself when you have done particularly well. It will make you feel better and more motivated.

When people receive rewards for a job well done, they tend to be more motivated and have the determination to repeat certain behaviours again so they get to experience the reward again, right? As the time flies, you will notice that you have already overcome the bad trait and you are able to move into better behaviour in replacement of the old one. You become motivated and determined because you know that even though you know how hard it is to keep yourself from certain bad habits, at the end of the day, a reward is waiting for you.

You must remember that, for a reward to be successful in overcoming that bad habit, it should be consistent and make sure that the value of the reward is proportional to your wants and desires. Once you are used to receiving rewards for your progress, it becomes an expectation and therefore a normality. Without realising it, you are likely to find that many of your subconscious acts and thoughts are geared towards receiving the reward without it being preoccupied with the habit.

QUICK PLAN

- **Identify key milestones in your plan and decide what you might do to reward yourself for reaching them**

- **Don't forget to celebrate each step forward that you make, even if it is just to congratulate yourself.**

BE NICE TO YOURSELF

STEP SIXTEEN

Be Nice to Yourself

*Holding onto anger is like grasping a hot coal
with the intent of throwing it at someone else;
you are the one who gets burned.*

Buddha

Bad habits often develop because of the lack of forgiveness for ourselves, others or even circumstances at some point in our lives. Sometimes habits are formed from experiences which have really hurt us and we allow them to continue to do so.   Perhaps we started drinking heavily out of anger, stress or despair.   It is common with a lot of habits.   We start them because of some negative experience.

Moving forward would be a very difficult course to consider if one fails to recognise the importance of forgiving.

Importance of forgiving

To forgive is our choice.

It requires an open heart and a deeper awareness of the mind. Quite simply, you cannot change the past. So why think about it and let it affect your future? By allowing your anger for the past to remain you are simply allowing it to stay alive and affect your life right now and, very probably, into the future. How crazy is that?

Theresa was so angry that her parents had died when she was young. She blamed herself for not loving them enough, the medical profession who could not save them from the horrific accident that they had been involved and the other driver for being involved in the accident. She blamed everyone she could think of because she had held onto the pain for decades. It lived with her every single day of her life.

To subdue the pain she started to neglect herself. She started smoking, drinking heavily and maintained a very poor diet of take away foods and pre-cooked meals.

Her health was deteriorating, she couldn't hold down a successful relationship and her work suffered because she was constantly turning up late or couldn't focus because of a heavy drinking session or something similar.

Who suffered as a consequence? Of course! She did!

What did the anger, bitterness, holding onto the past actually bring her. Nothing but more of the same.

I have had clients who have had held onto self-destructive thoughts and habits because of something that they no longer had any control over whatsoever. Very often, when I've explored the actual root cause with them in some detail we have found that the event or circumstance did not deserve the level of attention that it had been given.

Once they have been able to forgive themselves and others for incidents long past it has been like a heavy cloud being lifted from them and they have been able to rebuild their lives to become much fuller and productive. This, in itself, gave them much more hope about the beauty that exists rather than the dark past they had been stuck in.

Learn from mistakes

One particular attribute that defines humans is the ability to commit mistakes. We were all born with some level of imperfection. Human nature often leads us to stumble and screw things up from time to time. It's sad to hear, but this is just the reality of us being "human" – we make mistakes. Yet, being "human" also entitles us to a very interesting ability to learn from our shortcomings.

We have the capacity to learn and understand why these things happen. We also learn to change our behaviour and thoughts to do things differently the next time. It is our ability to learn and adapt that has made us so successful as a species:

1. *Forgiveness is a chance of growing*
   We grow when we commit mistakes. That is to say, rather than allowing ourselves to wallow in the grounds of committing mistakes, we can learn the important lessons that we need for us to grow. We should never think that forgiving is committing yet another mistake. Rather, we could consider it as a means to learn another very essential lesson in life, that to forgive is actually to move our lives forward.

2. *Forgiveness is an avenue to learn and unlearn things*
   We can manage our very own perception of the things that happen in our lives. We learn and become more knowledgeable. Along with this learning, we should also take it as

an opportunity to unlearn our bad aspects, our bad behaviours. We can unlearn hatred, pride and self-centeredness. Instead, we could sow in the seeds of love, humility and compassion.

3. *Forgivingness helps us become stronger*
Maybe you were wrong when you did not accept his sincere apology. Perhaps we were wrong when we fail to say sorry to those people we hurt. Perhaps we failed to realise that we were wrong, very wrong.

Admitting that we're wrong and allowing reconciliation to occur are just two things of an important whole. You see, forgiving is not always about being weak, but far greater than that, it is more about becoming brave and stronger – just as Mahatma Gandhi once said, "Forgiveness is the attitude of the strong."

In case of a slip up
Accept it; we slip up many times over many things. Who cares? It is an undeniable part of life. Even science has not yet perfected an invention that attributes virtually zero error. So it's true of human beings. None of us can expected to be error-free.

Alexander Pope once said, "To err is human, to forgive is divine." We have our weaknesses, we experience sadness, we grieve over losses, we feel thirsty, hungry and we get sickness. But one great step that can, at some point, improve our well-being, is when we pop sufficient pills of forgiveness.

In short, folks, we should learn to forgive and prepare to embrace a much happier, healthier future rather than holding onto the dark and distant memories of long ago.

That forgiveness starts with yourself. Ease up a bit and stop beating yourself up. Learn how things can change if you want a more successful future. Learn to make peace with yourself and others.

QUICK PLAN

- **Reframe any negative thoughts that you might find you're thinking into the positive**

- **If you slip up and revert back to the habit at any point DO NOT beat yourself up. Simply go back to step one and work yourself through the process.**

CONCLUSION

Conclusion

Congratulations in finishing this book. I hope you have learned a lot and have already discovered how to control and change your bad habits. It is my goal to equip you with the things you need to know so you can transform your life for the better.

I am grateful that you have allowed me to be part of your journey.

Do what is right and try to live right. If at first you don't succeed, dust yourself off and try again!

Don't lose hope or be disheartened. Fight back and be free from the bad habits that hinder your pathway to success. Make it happen! I know you can do it.

If you want to learn more about how you can Smash that habit, visit my website dedicated to this subject where you will find programmes designed to help you through the process.

Visit:

www.kulmahay.com

If you want to learn more about my work, please connect with me through any of the following:

www.facebook.com/kulmahayofficial
www.twitter.com/kulmahay
www.linkedin.com/in/kulmahay
www.instagram.com/kulmahay/

Finally, if you enjoyed this book, then I'd like to ask you for a favour. Would you be kind enough to leave a review for this book on Amazon? It'd be greatly appreciated!

Here's to you **smashing the habit!!**
Sending you love!

Kul

About The Author

Kul Mahay, is a Peak Performance Coach and Speaker. He works with leaders and business owners globally across a wide ssues.

He uses his own unique brand of 'Immersion Coaching' to get the lasting results from clients in the shortest possible time. He only deals with clients who are prepared to experience intense coaching and take massive action. If this sounds like you, get in touch.

26946140R00090

Printed in Great Britain
by Amazon